THE INVINCIBLE DEFENSE - COUNTER TO THE NARCISSIST'S PLAYBOOK

THE INVINCIBLE DEFENSE - COUNTER TO THE NARCISSIST'S PLAYBOOK

TINA R PAONE

TALL OAKS
PUBLISHING

The Invincible Defense: Counter to the Narcissist's Playbook

By Dr. Tina R. Paone
Edited by Jennifer S. Gabriel
Acknowledgments to Alex Romagnoli

Published by Tall Oaks Publishing
Lansdale, PA
ISBN: 979-8-9944043-3-1
Printed in the United States of America
First Edition

CONTENTS

Disclaimer and Safety Notice

The information provided in this Book is for informational and educational purposes only. It is not intended to be a substitute for professional mental health counseling, medical advice, or legal services. The content within this book should not be used to diagnose or treat any condition.

This playbook uses football terminology strictly as a metaphor to describe patterns of psychological manipulation and emotional abuse. It is not intended to reference, stereotype, or disparage football players, coaches, teams, or the sport itself. Football is used solely as a familiar strategic language to help clarify complex relational dynamics. The behaviors described are not inherent to athletics or football culture, and the intent is education—not judgment.

Immediate Safety Warning

If you are in immediate danger, fear for your safety, or are in an emergency situation, please stop reading and contact your local emergency services (such as 911), a trusted support system, or a domestic violence hotline immediately (800-799-7233 or text "BEGIN" to 88788.)

Personal Responsibility

Every individual's situation is unique and potentially high-risk. You must assess your own circumstances and safety before enacting any suggestions or strategies mentioned in this book. The author and publisher assume no responsibility for any actions taken or consequences resulting from the application of the information provided herein.

Safety Planning

The suggestions in this book are most effective when integrated into a comprehensive, personalized safety plan. We strongly encourage you to work with a trained advocate or professional to develop a plan that addresses your specific needs and environment.

How to Read this Playbook

The first playbook, *Recognize the Cadence: The Narcissist's Offensive Playbook,* was written to help you see the game clearly—to recognize the patterns, language, and tactics used to control, confuse, and destabilize. This playbook exists for what comes next.

Once you can see the plays, the work shifts from understanding them to protecting you. This isn't a book about confrontation or changing the narcissist. It's a defensive playbook—built for nervous-system safety, clear limits, and decisions that reduce access. The goal is simple: stop giving up ground, reclaim your reality, and leave the game on your terms.

You don't need to read this book in order. Go directly to the play that matches what you're facing now. Each defensive chapter corresponds to a specific offensive play from the first book, so recognition can quickly become action. You don't need to master every defense to be protected—one clear response, applied consistently at the right moment, is often enough.

In narcissistic systems, you were likely rewarded for explaining yourself, staying calm under pressure, being reasonable, or handling things "the right way." This book does not ask you to perform. The defenses here are designed to work even when you're tired, dysregulated, or unsure—simple, grounded responses that protect your energy and your clarity.

Teams

Every game has two sides. If you read the first playbook, *Recognize the Cadence: The Narcissist's Offensive Playbook,* you know that in narcissistic systems, understanding who is on the field—and what role they play—helps explain why the same dynamics repeat, even when you change your behavior. Here's a recap:

The Offensive Unit (The Narcissistic System)

In a narcissistic abuse system, the Offensive Unit is designed to advance power, avoid accountability, and keep control of the game.

The Narcissist is the Quarterback (QB). This is the central decision-maker who controls the ball and calls every play. They decide who is targeted, how the play unfolds, and when to pivot, all while demanding loyalty and obedience.

The Primary Victim is the Ball. The goal is not partnership but possession. The Ball does not choose where it goes; it is moved, controlled, passed, or sacrificed to advance the play. Every action on the field revolves around controlling the Ball. (Note: This metaphor reflects the narcissist's mindset—not your worth, agency, or humanity.)

Blocking Backs / Fullbacks represent Enablers, also known as "Flying Monkeys". Their job is to clear the path for the Quarterback, ignoring challenges, absorbing impact, and protecting the play. Many are unaware they're playing this role, believing they're "helping," "keeping the peace," or that the Quarterback narrative is reality.

Offensive Linemen (Center, Guards, Tackles) represent Structural Enablers, also known as an Emotional Shield. They form the wall directly in front of the Quarterback, absorbing pressure and preventing defenders (truth, accountability, consequences) from getting through. These can be family systems, workplace hierarchies, legal structures, or social norms that protect the narcissist by design, not intent.

Wide Receivers and Tight Ends represent Distraction Enablers. They run decoy routes—spreading misinformation, shifting focus, or creating side conflicts—to pull attention away from the abuse itself. Their role is confusion, misdirection, and plausible deniability, often without realizing they are part of the play.

Together, the Offensive Unit ensures one outcome: The Quarterback stays protected, the Ball stays controlled, and accountability never reaches the backfield.

The Defensive Unit (Reality and Truth)

If the Offensive Unit exists to protect control, the Defensive Unit exists to restore reality. This is the opposition: the side of the field committed to truth, safety, and long-term healing.

The Head Coach represents Therapists and Counselors. As master strategists, they teach the defensive player how the opponent actually operates by breaking down the Narcissist's Playbook (the abuse cycle). They call timeouts through scheduled sessions and intentional rest, helping regulate the nervous system and prevent burnout. Their ultimate goal isn't to win a single play—it's to prepare the player for the decisive play: the Interception, often experienced as No Contact or firm, enforced boundaries.

The Defensive Coordinator represents a Trusted Support Network. These are the family and friends who hold reality steady. They provide grounding between drives, reinforce what actually happened, and restore morale when the victim has been benched through devaluation or self-doubt. Their role is not strategy but stabilization: reminding the defender of their worth, strength, and sanity when the noise gets loud.

The Film Analyst represents Education and Research. This is the process of studying game tape—learning about narcissistic abuse, trauma bonding, gaslighting, and coercive control. By reviewing past plays, patterns become visible. The chaos stops feeling personal and starts looking predictable. Knowledge doesn't stop the offense, but it removes the element of surprise—and that changes the entire game.

Together, the Defensive Unit does what the offense cannot tolerate: it names reality, slows the game down, and makes escape not just possible, but sustainable. If you don't have all of these roles yet, start with one: a single safe person, a single education source, or a single therapist who helps you hold reality steady.

Object of the Game (And What Winning Really Means)

The object of the game is not to defeat the narcissist, prove a point, or force accountability. The object is to protect your reality, reclaim your agency, and heal. Winning is not measured by how the narcissist responds, but by how much control they lose over your time, energy, and sense of self.

In narcissistic systems, knowledge works the same way it does in football. When you can recognize patterns—both after the play and in real time—you can choose a defense that fits the moment instead of reacting on impulse.

Anticipation matters. Just as a player who studies game film can jump a route before the ball is thrown, understanding narcissistic patterns allows you to see where the play is headed and respond before you're pulled in.

Discipline matters even more. Narcissistic offenses rely on bait—provocation, urgency, emotional pressure—to create mental errors. When you refuse to take the bait and hold your ground, one of two things happens: the narcissist escalates and reveals the play more clearly, or they retreat to regroup. Either way, you stop giving up easy yards.

You do not win by playing harder. A "win" occurs whenever you interrupt the pattern and stop advancing the narcissist's drive.

Win Condition #1: Recognizing the Play

This is the first and most essential victory. You identify the tactic for what it is—love bombing, gaslighting, blame shifting—without minimizing it or personalizing it. Recognition alone weakens the play, because confusion is the offense's greatest advantage.

Win Condition #2: Holding Reality

Here, you trust your memory, perception, and emotional response, even when they are challenged or dismissed. You stop debating your reality and refuse to surrender your internal truth. Each time you hold your ground internally, the offense loses leverage.

Win Condition #3: Enforcing a Boundary

A boundary is not an argument or an explanation—it is a limit followed by action. When you enforce a boundary, you reclaim territory the narcissist was using to control you. Whether the boundary is respected or punished, the win is that you held it.

Win Condition #4: Disengaging from the Play

This is a decisive defensive stop. You choose not to respond, not to react, and not to continue the exchange. Disengagement ends the drive.

Win Condition #5: Ending the Game

This is the final victory. Through distance, no contact, or firm structural boundaries, the narcissist loses access entirely. The game clock runs out. Healing, peace, and freedom become possible because the offense can no longer take the field.

How This Playbook Is Structured

Each counter in this section corresponds directly to a specific offensive play outlined in *Recognize the Cadence: The Narcissist's Offensive Playbook.* The order and numbering are intentional, allowing you to move easily between the two books as recognition turns into response.

Each counter in this playbook is built to help you move from recognition to response without getting pulled into over-explaining or emotional labor. Every section follows the same structure:

What It Is
A clear definition of the play—naming the behavior without minimizing or dramatizing it.

Penalty
What the play costs you if it continues in terms of clarity, safety, agency, energy, or stability.

Defensive Counter
What to do when the play shows up, stated as a simple, repeatable phrase.

On-Field Adjustments
The snaps are common lines you'll hear under pressure. The responses are designed to interrupt the pattern, protect your nervous system, and stop the drive—not to convince the narcissist.

Additional Defensive Moves
Practical actions that reinforce the counter: limits, pacing, documentation, support, and disengagement.

Why This Works
A concise explanation of why the counter disrupts the narcissistic system and protects your nervous system.

You don't need perfect execution. You need consistency. A clear boundary, applied repeatedly, stops more drives than a flawless speech ever will. Often these Defensive Counters will cause an escalation of the behavior. That is important information. It tells you that the defense is working.

Play #1 - Love Bombing

What It Is

Love bombing is the use of excessive attention, affection, flattery, gifts, or grand gestures early in a relationship to create rapid emotional attachment before trust, mutuality, or time can be established.

Penalty

Love bombing accelerates attachment through intensity rather than connection, creating a bond that feels intoxicating but remains shallow, conditional, and designed for control, not intimacy.

Defensive Counter

When closeness feels rushed, slow the game down: maintain pace, reduce access, and let time—not intensity—reveal character.

On-Field Adjustments

<u>Snap</u>
"I want to spend every second of the day with you."

<u>The Strategy</u>
Eliminating your outside life under the guise of passion and devotion.

<u>Possible Response</u>
"I love our time together, but I have plans with my friends tonight. Balance is important to me."

<u>Snap</u>
"Everyone else in my life is so boring compared to you."

<u>The Strategy</u>
Early isolation through flattery, setting an unspoken rule that you must remain exceptional to keep your position.

<u>Possible Response</u>
"That's a shame. I actually find most people have something interesting about them if you look."

<u>Snap</u>
"You're my soulmate—even if you are a bit much sometimes."

<u>The Strategy</u>
To deliver a "backhanded" compliment that makes you feel lucky to be "tolerated."

<u>Possible Response</u>
Don't defend the insult. Just address the behavior: "That's a weird way to pay a compliment."

<u>Snap</u>
"I bought you this expensive gift after only two dates."

<u>The Strategy</u>
This is a silent gesture that carries immense weight. They aren't saying you owe them, but the gift creates a debt you didn't ask for and pressure to fall in line for the rest of the drive.

<u>Possible Response</u>
"This is a beautiful gift, but it's a bit much. Let's keep things simple while we're getting to know each other."

<u>Snap</u>
"I've never told anyone this before, but my childhood was really hard... I feel safe with you."

<u>The Strategy</u>
Creating emotional debt through premature vulnerability to prompt reciprocal disclosure.

<u>Possible Response</u>
"I appreciate you sharing that with me; that sounds like it was really difficult. I'm a bit more private, so I like to wait until I really know someone before I dive into my own past."

<u>Snap</u>
"I was just thinking about you—did you feel it? I feel like our souls are tethered."

<u>The Strategy</u>
Using constant contact to collapse space, accelerate emotional dependency, and crowd out your internal and external supports.

<u>Possible Response</u>
"I love hearing from you, and I'm going off the grid for a few hours to focus on work/self-care. I'll check back in with you this evening."

Additional Defensive Moves
- Set communication limits ("I'm not available to text all day.")
- Decline early exclusivity or commitment ("I move slowly and build trust over time.")
- Maintain routines, friendships, and independent plans
- Redirect future-focused promises back to the present ("Let's focus on getting to know each other.")
- Take note of expensive gifts or favors that create pressure or obligation

Why This Works
Love bombing collapses under time because a healthy connection can tolerate pacing, while a controlling dynamic relies on speed to bypass discernment.

Play #2 - Gaslighting

What It Is
Gaslighting is a manipulation tactic in which the narcissist denies, distorts, or rewrites reality to make you question your memory, perception, or sanity, shifting authority away from your lived experience and onto theirs.

Penalty
Gaslighting erodes trust in your own mind, creating confusion, self-doubt, and emotional exhaustion that keeps you dependent on the narcissist as the sole "reliable" source of truth.

Defensive Counter
When your reality is repeatedly questioned or rewritten, stop debating the facts: trust your perception, state your truth once, and disengage from arguments about what "really" happened.

On-Field Adjustments
<u>Snap</u>
"I never said that. You're remembering it wrong."

<u>The Strategy</u>
Erasing prior conversations to avoid accountability and destabilize your confidence in your memory.

<u>Possible Response</u>
"I know what I heard, and I'm not going to argue about my memory."

<u>Snap</u>
"You're too sensitive—you're overreacting."

<u>The Strategy</u>
Shifting focus from their behavior to your reaction so you question your emotional legitimacy instead of their actions.

<u>Possible Response</u>
"My reaction makes sense based on what happened."

<u>Snap</u>

"That's not how it played out. Your head isn't in the game lately."

<u>The Strategy</u>

Questioning your mental clarity to invalidate your perception and avoid accountability.

<u>Possible Response</u>

"My memory is actually very clear on this. I don't need you to tell me how I experienced that moment."

Additional Defensive Moves

- Keep written records, screenshots, or notes to ground yourself privately
- Reality-check with trusted people in your support system
- Refuse circular arguments about intent, tone, or memory
- End conversations that devolve into confusion or self-defense
- Anchor decisions in patterns, not explanations

Why This Works

Gaslighting depends on engagement and self-doubt; when you stop arguing about reality and remove the narcissist's role as referee, the tactic loses its power.

Play #3 - Hoovering

What It Is

Hoovering is an attempt to re-establish contact and control after distance or separation through charm, guilt, apology, crisis, or sudden declarations of change.

Penalty

Hoovering reactivates trauma bonds by exploiting hope, empathy, and unfinished emotional business, pulling you back into the cycle just as distance begins to restore clarity.

Defensive Counter

When contact resumes after distance and is driven by urgency, emotion, or promises of change, do not re-engage: maintain distance, limit access, and let behavior—not words—speak.

On-Field Adjustments

Snap
"I've changed. I finally understand everything now."

The Strategy
Rewriting history and offering insight without accountability to regain access.

Possible Response
No response.

Snap
"I'm really struggling—I don't know who else to turn to."

The Strategy
Triggering empathy and responsibility to pull you back into emotional care-taking.

Possible Response
"I hope you find the support you need." (Then disengage.)

Additional Defensive Moves

- Maintain no contact or strictly limited contact
- Do not respond to emotional bait, apologies, or crises

- Revisit documented patterns before responding
- Use third-party or structured communication if contact is unavoidable
- Anchor decisions in past behavior, not present promises

Why This Works

Hoovering depends on renewed access; when contact is denied and hope is replaced with clarity, the cycle cannot restart.

Play #4 - Projection

What It Is

Projection is the act of disowning one's own thoughts, traits, emotions, or behaviors and assigning them to someone else in order to avoid accountability and preserve a false self-image.

Penalty

Projection reverses responsibility, forcing you to defend against accusations that originate from the narcissist's own behavior, leaving you confused, defensive, and off-balance.

Defensive Counter

When accusations feel misplaced or eerily familiar, stop defending and redirect responsibility: name what is yours, refuse what is not, and disengage from the false exchange.

On-Field Adjustments

<u>Snap</u>
"You're the one who's always lying."

<u>The Strategy</u>
Offloading guilt and misconduct by accusing you of the very behavior they are engaging in.

<u>Possible Response</u>
"I'm comfortable with my integrity." (Do not debate.)

<u>Snap</u>
"You're obsessed with drama—you love conflict."

<u>The Strategy</u>
Assigning their volatility to you so you stop naming harm

<u>Possible Response</u>
"I'm choosing calm and distance." (End the interaction.)

<u>Snap</u>
"You always have to be in control—everything has to be your way."

<u>The Strategy</u>
Assigning their control tactics to you so you defend yourself instead of holding the line.

<u>Possible Response</u>
"I'm comfortable with my choices. If you want to discuss logistics, I'll be available Tuesday afternoon."

Additional Defensive Moves

- Stop explaining or disproving false accusations
- Identify patterns rather than arguing facts
- Use brief, neutral responses or silence
- Re-anchor yourself in observable behavior
- Exit conversations that become circular or accusatory

Why This Works

Projection collapses when responsibility is not accepted or returned; without your participation, the false narrative has nowhere to land.

Play #5 - Blame Shifting

What It Is

Blame shifting is the practice of redirecting responsibility for one's actions, reactions, or consequences onto another person in order to avoid accountability and maintain control.

Penalty

Blame shifting distorts cause and effect, conditioning you to accept responsibility for behavior you did not choose and outcomes you did not create.

Defensive Counter

When responsibility is immediately redirected to you after harm occurs, refuse the transfer: separate your behavior from theirs and do not accept accountability for their choices.

On-Field Adjustments

Snap
"I only did that because you pushed me to it."

The Strategy
Justifying harmful behavior by framing it as a reaction you caused.

Possible Response
"I am responsible for my actions, and you are responsible for yours. I didn't make you do anything."

Snap
"I'm owning my part—but you need to admit you started this."

The Strategy
Offering conditional accountability that still assigns primary fault to you.

Possible Response
"I'm clear on my part. I'm not taking responsibility for yours."

Snap
"You know how I get—why would you push that button?"

Training you to manage their emotions by avoiding topics, needs, or boundaries.

Possible Response
"I'm not responsible for managing your behavior." (End conversation.)

Additional Defensive Moves

- Decline debates about intent versus impact
- Refuse to justify, argue, or over-explain
- Restate responsibility once, then disengage
- Observe whether accountability is ever taken
- End conversations that revolve around assigning fault

Why This Works

Blame shifting requires your agreement to succeed; when responsibility is clearly defined and not absorbed, the manipulation loses traction.

Play #6 - Triangulation

What It Is

Triangulation introduces a third party—real or implied—to create insecurity, competition, or validation so power shifts back to the narcissist.

Penalty

Triangulation destabilizes your confidence and relationships by forcing you to perform, compare, or defend yourself against a moving target you can't verify.

Defensive Counter

When comparisons, "other people," or implied rivals enter the conversation, refuse the triangle: don't compete, don't chase validation, and bring the interaction back to direct reality—or disengage.

On-Field Adjustments

Snap
"Our mutual friend agrees with me that you're overreacting."

The Strategy
Using "crowd noise" to pressure you into compliance and make you doubt your perception.

Possible Response
"I'm not discussing this through other people. If you have something to say, say it directly."

Snap
"Why can't you be more like (person's name)?"

The Strategy
Creating competition to keep you proving your worth and chasing approval.

Possible Response
"I'm not going to compete with someone else for basic respect."

"My mother is going to love you so much more than my last girlfriend; she was so judgmental, not like you."

The Strategy
Using comparison to create insecurity and compliance while framing it as praise.

Possible Response
"I'm glad we get along well, but I don't like being compared to people from your past. Everyone has their own story."

Additional Defensive Moves
- Ask for direct communication only ("If it's important, talk to me—not about me.")
- Don't defend yourself to unnamed sources ("I'm not responding to anonymous opinions.")
- Reality-check with trusted supports outside the narcissistic system
- Limit disclosure about your relationships, insecurities, or "rivals"
- If a third party is involved, address it once, calmly, with facts—then disengage
- Reduce contact when triangulation becomes a recurring pattern

Why This Works
Triangulation collapses when you refuse to compete or litigate a third-party narrative—without your participation, the narcissist loses the leverage of comparison and confusion.

Play #7 - Silent Treatment

What It Is

The silent treatment is the deliberate withdrawal of communication, attention, or emotional presence in order to punish, control, or destabilize another person.

Penalty

The silent treatment weaponizes absence, creating anxiety, self-doubt, and urgency that pressures you to restore connection by apologizing, chasing, or abandoning your own needs.

Defensive Counter

When silence is used as punishment or leverage, stop chasing the connection: maintain your routines, ground yourself in reality, and do not reward withdrawal with pursuit.

On-Field Adjustments

Snap
(Days of silence after a disagreement)

The Strategy
Creating emotional distress to force you to re-engage on their terms.

Possible Response
No pursuit. Continue your life.

Snap
"I have nothing to say to you right now."

The Strategy
Withholding communication to assert dominance and provoke compliance.

Possible Response
"I'm available to talk when communication is respectful." (Then disengage.)

Additional Defensive Moves

- Resist the urge to explain, apologize, or chase
- Anchor yourself in external reality and support

- Document patterns of withdrawal
- Set expectations for healthy communication
- Treat prolonged silence as information, not mystery

Why This Works

The silent treatment loses power when it no longer produces pursuit; without your reaction, withdrawal fails as a control tactic.

Play #8 - Devaluation

What It Is

Devaluation is the shift from idealizing you to systematically criticizing, humiliating, or dismissing you to erode confidence and increase control.

Penalty

Devaluation attacks self-worth over time, conditioning you to accept less, doubt yourself more, and work harder to earn basic kindness.

Defensive Counter

When respect drops and criticism becomes routine, stop trying to "earn" your place: name the standard, set a limit, and disengage from conversations that include contempt or humiliation.

On-Field Adjustments

Snap
"No one else would ever put up with you."

The Strategy
Undermining your confidence so you cling to them as your only option.

Possible Response
"That's not an acceptable way to speak to me. I'm ending this conversation."

Snap
"You always mess things up—I should've just handled it myself."

The Strategy
Undermining your competence to justify control and reduce your confidence.

Possible Response
"That's disrespectful. I'm ending this conversation."

Snap
"You're exhausting. Everything with you is always a problem."

Pathologizing your needs so you stop expressing them.

"I won't be spoken to that way. We can revisit this later if it's respectful."

"I'm just joking—why can't you take a joke?"

Disguising contempt as humor so you doubt your right to object.

"I don't stay in conversations where I'm mocked." (Then disengage.)

Additional Defensive Moves

- Identify contempt early: insults, sarcasm, mocking, "jokes" that cut you down
- Limit emotional disclosure to someone who weaponizes vulnerability
- Re-anchor in external reality: trusted supports, therapy, written reminders of truth
- Set a clear rule: no discussion in the presence of disrespect
- Track patterns (frequency, triggers, escalation) to guide decisions
- Increase distance if devaluation persists—especially after boundaries are stated

Why This Works

Devaluation relies on your continued engagement and self-doubt; when access and attention are no longer rewarded under contempt, the tactic loses its payoff.

Play #9 - Smear Campaign

What It Is

A smear campaign is the deliberate spread of false, exaggerated, or misleading information to damage your credibility, isolate you from support, and preempt accountability.

Penalty

Smear campaigns undermine reputation and trust, forcing you into a defensive position where energy is spent disproving lies instead of protecting yourself.

Defensive Counter

When your character is attacked behind your back, do not chase the narrative: stay anchored in truth, limit explanations, and allow consistency—not defense—to restore credibility.

On-Field Adjustments

Snap
"I'm really worried about them—they're unstable."

The Strategy
Framing concern to disguise character assassination and isolate you from allies.

Possible Response
No public rebuttal. (Address concerns privately with trusted friends only.)

Snap
"They're the real abuser. I'm the victim."

The Strategy
Role reversal to discredit you before accountability can reach them.

Possible Response
No public rebuttal.

Snap
"She's crazy. She's overreacting to nothing."

<u>The Strategy</u>

By labeling your reaction as "too much," they shift the focus from their behavior to your "unsportsmanlike conduct." They want others to see you as unstable rather than apologizing for their behavior.

<u>Possible Response</u>
No public rebuttal.

Additional Defensive Moves

- Resist the urge to defend yourself or facts
- Maintain consistent, grounded behavior over time
- Share truth selectively with safe people
- Document patterns in case clarification is later required
- Accept that some people may believe the smear

Why This Works

Smear campaigns collapse under consistency; when you stop feeding the narrative and remain steady, false stories lose momentum.

Play #10 - Playing the Victim

What It Is

Playing the victim is the strategic adoption of helplessness, injury, or persecution to gain sympathy, avoid accountability, and redirect attention away from harmful behavior.

Penalty

Weaponized victimhood reverses roles, positioning you as the aggressor and forcing you to defend yourself while the narcissist escapes responsibility.

Defensive Counter

When accountability is met with fragility or collapse, do not rescue or reassure: acknowledge feelings without accepting blame, and return focus to behavior and boundaries.

On-Field Adjustments

Snap
"You're always attacking me—I can't handle this."

The Strategy
Shifting the focus from their behavior to your tone or delivery.

Possible Response
"I'm discussing behavior, not attacking you." (Then disengage.)

Snap
"After everything I've done for you, this is how you treat me?"

The Strategy
Using guilt and sacrifice to invalidate your needs.

Possible Response
"I'm allowed to have needs."

Additional Defensive Moves

- Avoid over-apologizing or care-taking
- Separate empathy from responsibility

- Keep boundaries firm during emotional displays
- Notice patterns of collapse following accountability
- End conversations that center their suffering over your safety

Why This Works

Playing the victim fails when it no longer secures reassurance or exemption; without rescue, the tactic loses its leverage.

Play #11 - Future Faking

What It Is

Future faking is the use of grand promises, plans, or commitments to secure present compliance without any genuine intention of follow-through.

Penalty

Future faking trades hope for control, keeping you emotionally invested in a future that never arrives while present behavior remains unchanged.

Defensive Counter

When promises replace action, shift focus to the present: stop investing in potential and assess behavior as it exists now.

On-Field Adjustments

Snap
"Once things settle down, everything will be different."

The Strategy
Postponing accountability with vague future relief.

Possible Response
"I need consistency now, not promises later."

Snap
"I'm already looking at houses for us. I can see our kids having your eyes."

The Strategy
Overwhelming you with a fully imagined future before the present relationship has been tested. By filling in a fantasy that mirrors your hopes, they collapse discernment and replace evaluation with emotional momentum.

Possible Response
"I love that we have a vision for the future, but I want to make sure we enjoy the present first. Let's take our time getting to know each other in the here and now."

Snap
"I'm going to marry you—I just need more time."

<u>The Strategy</u>
Securing commitment without delivering stability.

<u>Possible Response</u>
Silence. (Observe actions.)

Additional Defensive Moves

- Measure consistency, not intention
- Stop making sacrifices based on future payoff
- Anchor decisions in current behavior
- Revisit patterns of broken promises
- Reduce emotional investment when action stalls

Why This Works

Future faking collapses when hope is replaced with observation; without belief in the promise, the leverage disappears.

Play #12 - Boundary Testing

What It Is

Boundary testing involves repeated, incremental violations of stated limits to assess how much resistance exists and how far control can be extended. These violations often appear minor, reasonable, or accidental—but they are deliberate probes. Each test asks the same question: *Will you enforce the line, or will I get more access if I push?*

Boundary testing rarely starts with overt defiance. It begins with small oversteps that seem easier to excuse than confront, slowly shifting the baseline of what you tolerate.

Penalty

Boundary testing erodes safety and self-trust by normalizing small violations until limits no longer feel enforceable. Over time, you may begin to doubt your right to have boundaries at all—or feel exhausted by the constant need to defend them. What began as a clear line turns into a moving target, and control expands quietly.

Defensive Counter

When boundaries are tested rather than respected, respond consistently: restate the limit once, enforce it with action, and then disengage.

On-Field Adjustments

Snap
"I know you said not to call late, but this is important."

The Strategy
Framing violations as exceptions to weaken limits.

Possible Response
"I'm in bed. We can talk in the morning."

Snap
"You're being too rigid."

The Strategy
Shaming boundaries to regain access.

Possible Response
"This boundary isn't negotiable."

<u>Snap</u>
"It was just one time—why are you making this such a big deal?"

<u>The Strategy</u>
Minimizing the violation so you doubt whether enforcement is 'worth it.'

<u>Possible Response</u>
"I'm enforcing the boundary we already discussed."

<u>Snap</u>
"I forgot—you know I'm bad with rules."

<u>The Strategy</u>
Claiming incompetence or innocence to avoid accountability and test whether consequences will follow.

<u>Possible Response</u>
"The boundary still applies." (Then enforce it.)

Additional Defensive Moves
- Avoid justifying or debating boundaries
- Enforce consequences immediately
- If they call late again: Do not answer. Return the call during your stated hours.
- If they show up unannounced: Do not open the door.
- If they keep texting after you set a limit: Mute/block for 24 hours.

Why This Works
Boundary testing fails when limits are consistently enforced; without flexibility to exploit, control attempts lose momentum.

Play #13 - Word Salad

What It Is

Word salad is the deliberate use of chaotic, circular, contradictory, or overwhelming communication to derail conversations and prevent accountability. It may sound intelligent, emotional, urgent, or pseudo-logical—but its function is not communication. Its function is confusion. Facts are blurred, topics shift mid-sentence, and no resolution is ever reached—because resolution is the one outcome the narcissistic system cannot tolerate.

Penalty

Word salad exhausts and disorients, leaving you confused, doubting yourself, and focused on clarity instead of safety.

Defensive Counter

When conversations become chaotic or incoherent, stop engaging: disengage from the dialogue and ground yourself in observable facts.

On-Field Adjustments

Snap
"That's not what we're talking about—you're twisting everything."

The Strategy
Abrupt topic shifts and accusations to reset the conversation and avoid accountability.

Possible Response
"This conversation isn't productive. I'm ending it." (Then disengage.)

Snap
"You said this—but actually you meant that—and if you hadn't done the other thing, none of this would matter anyway."

The Strategy
Flooding the exchange with contradictions so you lose the thread and doubt your own understanding.

<u>Possible Response</u>
Silence. (Exit the exchange.)

Additional Defensive Moves
- Refuse to chase clarity in chaos
- End conversations that lose structure
- Write down key facts privately
- Use brief, grounding statements
- Take physical or emotional distance

Why This Works
Word salad only works when you stay engaged long enough to lose your footing. The moment you stop participating, the tactic collapses. Without your attention and effort to "make sense" of it, chaos loses its leverage—and you regain control of your reality.

Play #14 - Baiting

What It Is

Baiting often masquerades as curiosity, bluntness, humor, or "truth-telling," but its function is the same: to pull you out of regulation and into defense. The goal is not honesty, resolution, or communication—it is activation. Once you react, the focus shifts away from their behavior and onto your tone, intensity, or emotions.

Penalty

Baiting reframes the interaction so your reaction becomes the problem. The original issue disappears, replaced by accusations about your anger, sensitivity, or instability. Over time, this conditions you to suppress emotion, over-monitor yourself, or stay silent—while the narcissist escapes accountability entirely.

Defensive Counter

When provocation is obvious, do not react: remain neutral, disengage, and deny the emotional payoff. You are not required to defend your feelings, clarify your tone, or prove your calm. The absence of reaction is the defense.

On-Field Adjustments

Snap
"Why are you so angry?"

The Strategy
Provoking emotion, then pathologizing the response.

Possible Response
No response.

Snap
"I'm just telling the truth."

The Strategy
Masking cruelty as transparency so your hurt becomes the issue instead of their intent.

Possible Response
"This conversation is over."

<u>Snap</u>
Sarcasm, smirking, eye-rolling, or mocking comments delivered just under the belt

<u>The Strategy</u>
Nonverbal bait meant to provoke without leaving verbal evidence.

<u>Possible Response</u>
Remove yourself from the environment.

Additional Defensive Moves

- Pause before responding
- Reduce emotional disclosure
- Leave the environment if needed
- Avoid explaining reactions
- Re-anchor in calm, not correctness

Why This Works

Baiting fails without reaction; neutrality removes the reward.

Play #15 - Playing Dumb

What It Is

Playing dumb is the strategic feigning of ignorance, confusion, or incompetence to avoid responsibility and shift effort, labor, or blame onto you. It often appears passive, harmless, or even self-deprecating—but it is not accidental. It is selective.

Penalty

Strategic incompetence drains energy and reinforces unequal labor, training you to over-function while the narcissist under-functions. Over time, you may feel resentful, exhausted, and trapped in a dynamic where responsibility always lands on you—not because you agreed to it, but because you were conditioned to "pick up the slack."

Defensive Counter

When confusion is performative, stop compensating: return responsibility to its rightful owner and disengage.

On-Field Adjustments

<u>Snap</u>
"I don't know how to do that—you're better at it."

<u>The Strategy</u>
Shifting responsibility while appearing helpless.

<u>Possible Response</u>
"You'll need to figure out another way."

<u>Snap</u>
"I have no idea what you're talking about—I don't remember any of that."

<u>The Strategy</u>
Avoiding accountability through feigned confusion.

<u>Possible Response</u>
"Then I'll give you some time to review." (Then disengage.)."

<u>Snap</u>
"You didn't explain it clearly—I can't do anything if you don't tell me exactly how."

Forcing you into over-explaining so responsibility quietly transfers to you.

Possible Response
"I've already explained it. It's your responsibility to follow through."

Additional Defensive Moves

- Stop rescuing or over-explaining
- Assign responsibility clearly
- Allow consequences to occur
- Notice patterns of selective confusion
- Reduce involvement when effort is avoided

Why This Works

Playing dumb only works when you compensate for it. When rescue stops, the tactic collapses. Responsibility either returns to its rightful owner—or the cost of avoidance becomes visible. Either outcome restores balance and protects your energy.

Play #16 - Isolation

What It Is

Isolation is the systematic discouragement or disruption of your relationships, support systems, and external connections in order to increase dependence and control. It rarely begins with outright bans. More often, it shows up as criticism, guilt, subtle sabotage, or repeated "concern" about the people and activities that keep you grounded.

Penalty

Isolation weakens reality testing and resilience. As external perspectives disappear, manipulation becomes harder to detect and easier to internalize. You may begin to doubt your instincts, feel guilty for wanting connection, or fear that maintaining relationships will "cause problems." Over time, isolation increases emotional dependence and reduces perceived exit options.

Defensive Counter

When outside relationships are criticized or restricted, protect your connections: maintain contact, resist guilt, and expand support rather than shrinking it.

On-Field Adjustments

Snap
"Your friends are a bad influence."

The Strategy
Undermining external support to increase dependence.

Possible Response
"My relationships matter to me."

Snap
"Why do you need them when you have me?"

The Strategy
Framing exclusivity as intimacy.

Possible Response
"I value more than one source of connection."

<u>Snap</u>
"They don't really care about you like I do."

<u>The Strategy</u>
Positioning themselves as the only safe or trustworthy attachment.

<u>Possible Response</u>
"That's not for you to decide."

Additional Defensive Moves
- Schedule regular contact with trusted people
- Share concerns with safe supports
- Notice patterns of jealousy or discouragement
- Resist pressure to choose sides
- Increase independence rather than reduce it

Why This Works
Connection is not the problem; it is the antidote. When your relationships remain intact, reality stays grounded and resilience increases. Support systems restore perspective, interrupt manipulation, and remind you who you were before the field narrowed.

Play #17 - Intermittent Reinforcement

What It Is

Intermittent reinforcement is the unpredictable alternation between affection and harm—kindness and cruelty, warmth and withdrawal—used to create emotional dependency and sustain hope. The kindness is never consistent, never reliable, and never earned through mutual respect. It arrives just often enough to keep you invested. This pattern mirrors addiction conditioning: the nervous system learns to stay hyper-alert, waiting for the next moment of relief.

Penalty

Inconsistency conditions you to tolerate harm in exchange for rare moments of connection or approval. Over time, your baseline shifts. You stop expecting safety or stability and begin negotiating for scraps—interpreting brief kindness as proof of change while minimizing ongoing harm. The result is emotional exhaustion, self-doubt, and a deep attachment to the very cycle that's hurting you.

Defensive Counter

When affection becomes unpredictable, stop chasing relief: evaluate patterns instead of moments and reduce emotional investment.

On-Field Adjustments

Snap
Sudden kindness after prolonged cruelty

The Strategy
Resetting hope to restart the cycle.

Possible Response
Observe without re-engaging.

Snap
"See? I can be good to you."

The Strategy
Using crumbs as proof of change.

<u>Possible Response</u>
Silence.

<u>Snap</u>
Why can't you just enjoy it when things are good?"

<u>The Strategy</u>
Pressuring you to live in moments instead of patterns so accountability disappears.

<u>Possible Response</u>
"I pay attention to consistency." (Then disengage.)

Additional Defensive Moves

- Track behavior over time
- Resist emotional highs and lows
- Stabilize routines and expectations
- Stop negotiating for kindness
- Reduce exposure to volatility

Why This Works

Consistency, not intensity, is the measure of safety. Intermittent reinforcement only works when unpredictability controls your nervous system. When you stop responding to the highs—and stop collapsing after the lows—the conditioning weakens. Without emotional payoff, the cycle loses its grip.

Play #18 - Minimization

What It Is

Minimization is the deliberate downplaying of harm, impact, or severity to invalidate your experience and avoid accountability. It reframes real injury as exaggeration, overreaction, or misunderstanding—often delivered calmly, casually, or with apparent reasonableness.

Penalty

Minimization erodes trust in your own perceptions, teaching you to second-guess your reactions and silence yourself. Over time, you may stop naming harm altogether—believing that if it didn't meet someone else's threshold, it doesn't count. This creates internal conflict, emotional suppression, and increasing dependence on the narcissist's version of reality.

Defensive Counter

When harm is minimized, do not argue impact: affirm your experience internally and disengage from invalidation.

On-Field Adjustments

Snap
"It wasn't a big deal."

The Strategy
Dismissing harm to escape accountability.

Possible Response
"It mattered to me."

Snap
"You're too sensitive."

The Strategy
Pathologizing your reaction.

Possible Response
Disengage.

<u>Snap</u>
"You're blowing this way out of proportion."

<u>The Strategy</u>
Recasting harm as exaggeration so you shrink your response.

<u>Possible Response</u>
"I'm clear on how this affected me."

<u>Snap</u>
"I've done worse things to other people—this is nothing."

<u>The Strategy</u>
Normalizing harm by comparison so your experience is erased.

<u>Possible Response</u>
Silence.

Additional Defensive Moves

- Stop justifying emotional responses
- Validate yourself privately
- Document incidents
- Reduce disclosure to unsafe listeners
- Exit invalidating conversations

Why This Works

Minimization loses power when your reality is no longer negotiable.

Play #19 - Shaming

What It Is

Shaming is an identity-level attack designed to induce guilt, humiliation, and compliance. Unlike criticism, which targets behavior, shame targets *who you are*. It aims to collapse your sense of self so that resistance feels morally wrong and silence feels safer than self-defense.

Penalty

Shame attacks self-worth and autonomy. It increases silence, self-doubt, and dependence by making you believe that your needs, boundaries, or reactions are evidence of personal failure. Over time, shame trains you to self-censor, overcompensate, or accept mistreatment as deserved.

Defensive Counter

When shame is used, disengage immediately: refuse identity-based attacks and remove yourself from the exchange.

On-Field Adjustments

<u>Snap</u>
"You should be ashamed of yourself."

<u>The Strategy</u>
Inducing moral collapse to regain control.

<u>Possible Response</u>
No response.

<u>Snap</u>
"Everyone knows what you're really like."

<u>The Strategy</u>
Leveraging fear of exposure.

<u>Possible Response</u>
Exit the scene. Find a safe space for yourself.

<u>Snap</u>
"What kind of person even thinks like that?"

<u>The Strategy</u>
Framing your thoughts or needs as evidence of defect or immorality.

<u>Possible Response</u>
"I'm not engaging with character attacks." (Then disengage.)

Additional Defensive Moves
- Name shame internally
- Reconnect with affirming voices
- Reduce vulnerability with unsafe people
- Reject global character attacks
- Increase emotional distance

Why This Works
Shame collapses when it is neither internalized nor engaged. Without your agreement, explanation, or defense, the attack has nowhere to land. Distance restores perspective—and perspective restores self-trust.

Play #20 - Entitlement

What It Is

Entitlement is the belief that one deserves special treatment, unrestricted access, or exemption from rules, boundaries, or consequences. It assumes superiority—of needs, feelings, time, or status—and treats other people's limits as inconveniences rather than realities.

Penalty

Entitlement normalizes exploitation and erases mutuality. Over time, your boundaries begin to feel optional, your needs secondary, and your refusal framed as cruelty or betrayal. The relationship becomes one-sided: accommodation flows in one direction, while accountability disappears in the other. Unchecked entitlement turns connection into obligation.

Defensive Counter

When entitlement appears, hold firm boundaries: do not accommodate demands that violate your limits or values.

On-Field Adjustments

Snap
"I shouldn't have to follow the same rules."

The Strategy
Asserting superiority to bypass limits.

Possible Response
"That doesn't work for me."

Snap
"You owe me."

The Strategy
Framing compliance as obligation.

Possible Response
"I hear you. And I disagree."

<u>Snap</u>
"After everything I've done for you, this is the least you can do."

<u>The Strategy</u>
Converting past actions into permanent leverage.

<u>Possible Response</u>
"Past choices don't give you control over my boundaries."

Additional Defensive Moves

- Treat demands as information
- Say no without justification
- Enforce consequences
- Notice patterns of exception-seeking

Why This Works

Entitlement depends on accommodation. Without special treatment, superiority collapses—and control attempts fail.

Play #21 - Rage / Explosive Anger

What It Is

Rage is designed to overwhelm your nervous system so fear—not reason—drives your response. It is the use of explosive anger—yelling, threats, intimidation, or physical presence—to silence opposition and reassert control. It is not a loss of control; it is a display of it. Rage is deployed when other tactics fail and the narcissistic system needs immediate compliance.

Penalty

Rage creates fear-based compliance and suppresses dissent. Over time, it conditions you to anticipate explosions, walk on eggshells, and self-censor to avoid escalation. The threat of rage becomes as controlling as rage itself, shrinking your world and eroding your sense of safety.

Defensive Counter

When anger escalates, prioritize safety over clarity, connection, or resolution. Disengage immediately and remove yourself from the situation. You are not required to de-escalate, explain, or soothe someone who is using rage as a weapon.

On-Field Adjustments

Snap
Yelling, threats, or intimidation

The Strategy
Using fear to dominate.

Possible Response
Leave the environment.

Snap
"You'll regret this."

The Strategy
Coercive threat.

Seek support.

Snap
"You're really pushing me—don't make me lose my temper."

The Strategy
Pre-emptive intimidation to make you responsible for their behavior.

Possible Response
"Let's talk about this in an hour."

Additional Defensive Moves

- End conversations at first escalation
- Create safety plans
- Document incidents
- Increase distance
- Involve outside support if needed

Why This Works

Rage only works when it produces submission. When fear no longer controls your decisions—when you leave, disengage, and protect yourself—the tactic loses its leverage. Without an audience or compliance, rage fails.

You do not owe anyone access to you at the expense of your safety. Anger can be communicated. Rage is a cue to leave.

Play #22 - Emotional Blackmail

What It Is

Emotional blackmail is the use of guilt, fear, threat, or manufactured crisis to force compliance. It creates a false equation: If you don't do what I want, something terrible will happen—and it will be your fault. This tactic exploits empathy and responsibility, positioning you as the regulator of another person's emotions, safety, or stability.

Penalty

Emotional blackmail traps you in responsibility for outcomes you do not control. It conditions you to prioritize another person's distress over your own safety, boundaries, and autonomy. Over time, this creates chronic anxiety, hypervigilance, and a belief that leaving, saying no, or enforcing limits is dangerous.

Blackmail doesn't just demand compliance—it demands self-erasure.

Defensive Counter

When compliance is demanded through fear or guilt, refuse responsibility and disengage. You are not obligated to sacrifice your safety, autonomy, or truth to prevent someone else's reaction. Threats are not needs. Fear is not consent.

On-Field Adjustments

Snap
"If you leave, I'll hurt myself."

The Strategy
Coercion through fear.

Possible Response
Contact emergency resources. Then disengage.

Snap
"A good partner would do this."

The Strategy
Moral pressure.

Possible Response
"That's not true."

<u>Snap</u>
"I can't survive without you."

<u>The Strategy</u>
Manufacturing dependence so your autonomy feels lethal.

<u>Possible Response</u>
Silence. (Do not assume responsibility.)

Additional Defensive Moves

- Do not negotiate under threat
- Involve third parties when safety is at risk
- Re-anchor responsibility
- Increase distance
- Prioritize protection over reassurance

Why This Works

Emotional blackmail collapses when coercion no longer dictates decisions. When threats are met with appropriate outside support—not compliance—the leverage disappears. Responsibility returns to its rightful place, and your autonomy is restored.

Play #23 - Warping Time

What It Is

Warping time is the deliberate distortion of timelines to invalidate memory, minimize harm, and evade responsibility. It collapses past, present, and future so accountability never fully lands. Events are dismissed as "too long ago," reframed as "just now," or rearranged to confuse cause and effect.

Penalty

Temporal distortion undermines trust in your own recollection and sense of continuity. When timelines are constantly rewritten, you may begin to doubt not just what happened, but when, how often, or whether it matters anymore. This erodes confidence, fuels self-doubt, and keeps you stuck arguing history instead of protecting yourself in the present.

When time is warped, patterns disappear—and without patterns, accountability dies.

Defensive Counter

When timelines are manipulated, stop debating chronology. Trust your memory, anchor yourself in facts and patterns, and disengage from arguments about timing. The question is not when it happened—it's that it happened.

On-Field Adjustments

Snap
"That happened years ago—get over it."

The Strategy
Erasing accountability.

Possible Response
"It still matters." (Then disengage.)

Snap
"I just said that yesterday."

The Strategy
Rewriting chronology.

Possible Response
Disengage.

Snap
"You're bringing up old stuff again—why can't you move on?"

The Strategy
Framing accountability as obsession so you stop naming patterns.

Possible Response
"I'm paying attention to patterns." (End the exchange.)

Snap
"That only happened once."

The Strategy
Isolating incidents so repeated behavior looks insignificant.

Possible Response
Silence. (Trust the pattern, not the claim.)

Additional Defensive Moves

- Keep records
- Anchor yourself in facts
- Stop arguing timelines
- Reduce disclosure
- Trust patterns

Why This Works

Warping time relies on negotiation—on your willingness to debate memory, dates, and relevance. When reality is no longer up for discussion, the tactic collapses. Patterns re-emerge, clarity returns, and your internal timeline stabilizes.

Play #24 - Grandiosity

What It Is

Grandiosity is the exaggerated sense of superiority that dismisses others' needs, pain, or humanity. It positions the narcissist as inherently more important, insightful, or deserving—while everyone else exists to reflect, support, or accommodate them.

In grandiosity, empathy is not merely absent; it is unnecessary. Other people's experiences are treated as distractions, inconveniences, or irrelevancies unless they serve the narcissist's self-image.

Penalty

Grandiosity enables emotional abandonment while maintaining proximity. You may still be present in the relationship, but your inner world is ignored, minimized, or erased. Over time, this teaches you to shrink your needs, stop expecting care, and internalize the belief that your pain matters less. The greatest harm of grandiosity is not cruelty—it is indifference.

Defensive Counter

When empathy is absent, stop seeking validation: disengage and protect your emotional energy.

On-Field Adjustments

Snap
"Your problems aren't that important."

The Strategy
Centering self at all costs so your needs disappear.

Possible Response
Withdraw emotionally. (Do not pursue validation.)

Snap
Blank stare, scrolling, dismissive silence, or changing the subject when you share something vulnerable

The Strategy
Emotional erasure—communicating that your inner world is irrelevant.

Possible Response
End disclosure. (Protect your interior.)

Snap
"I don't have time for this."

The Strategy
Declaring your needs unworthy of attention or care.

Possible Response
"Then this isn't the place for me to share." (Disengage.)

Snap
"You're making everything about you."

The Strategy
Accusing you of selfishness for having needs at all.

Possible Response
Silence. (Stop offering access.)

Additional Defensive Moves

- Lower expectations of empathy
- Seek validation elsewhere
- Reduce vulnerability
- Increase emotional distance
- Prioritize self-support

Why This Works

Grandiosity loses power when you recognize the false narrative.

Conclusion

This playbook was built for the moments when recognition isn't enough.

You can know exactly what play is being run—whether it's love bombing, gaslighting, rage, or hoovering—and still feel your body react like it's fourth-and-goal. That doesn't mean you're failing. It means you've been conditioned to play defense without a steady rulebook and to believe your job was to keep the peace no matter the cost.

But defense isn't about proving anything to the offense. It's about protecting what's yours.

Every time you slow the pace, hold your reality, enforce a boundary, or disengage from a trap, you stop giving up easy yards. You may not see it on the surface—especially if the narcissist escalates—but inside you, the game is changing. Your nervous system learns that you can survive the pressure. Your mind learns that you don't have to argue your way into being believed. Your life begins to expand again.

Some counters will feel simple. Some will feel impossibly hard. Both can be true. The goal isn't perfect execution—it's consistent protection. You don't need to run every defense. You need the one that fits the play you're facing, applied with clarity and repetition.

And if you take nothing else with you, take this:

A narcissist's greatest advantage is access. Your greatest strength is choice.

You get to decide what you engage, what you refuse, and what you leave behind. You get to choose reality over confusion, boundaries over bargaining, peace over performance. The offense may keep calling the same plays—but you are no longer playing blind.

You are building an invincible defense.

And when you're ready, you can walk off the field for good.

About the Author

Dr. Tina Paone is a licensed professional counselor, registered play therapist–supervisor, counselor educator, and tenured professor with more than 25 years of experience in the mental health field. Throughout her career, she has trained future therapists, led social justice initiatives, and supported survivors of complex trauma in reclaiming their lives.

Dr. Paone brings a rare dual lens to her work: deep clinical expertise paired with lived experience. In her forthcoming memoir, *UNBROKEN: Healing from Narcissistic Abuse and Reclaiming Me* (May 2026), she writes with clarity, authority, and compassion about surviving childhood grooming, emotional neglect, a coercive marriage, and post-separation abuse. The book is more than her story—it is a mirror for those still finding their voice.

Her current clinical focus centers on supporting survivors of narcissistic abuse and trauma-entrenched family systems. She is also a sought-after speaker and workshop facilitator whose work spans therapy, education, and advocacy.

She is also, fittingly, a lifelong Philadelphia Eagles fan, which means she believes in resilience, knows how to survive painful seasons, and never stops showing up, even when the game gets brutal.

Learn more about Dr. Paone's work—and subscribe to her newsletter—at drtinapaone.com.

www.ingramcontent.com/pod-product-compliance
Lightning Source LLC
Chambersburg PA
CBHW071210130626
46555CB00004B/1655